BATS!

STRANGE AND WONDERFUL

BY LAURENCE PRINGLE
ILLUSTRATED BY MERYL HENDERSON

Boyds Mills Press
Honesdale, Pennsylvania

For Kent Brown Jr. and fond memories of
pondering life's mysteries while eating
ice cream under Chautauqua's bat-dappled sky

—L.P.

To my husband, Jim, whose never-ending enthusiasm
for my work gives me great joy

—M.H.

Text copyright © 2000 by Laurence Pringle
Illustrations copyright © 2000 by Meryl Henderson

Boyds Mills Press, Inc.
815 Church Street
Honesdale, Pennsylvania 18431
Printed in China

Library of Congress Cataloging-in-Publication Data
Bats : strange and wonderful! / by Laurence Pringle ; illustrated by
Meryl Henderson.—1st ed.
   [32]p.: col. ill.;   cm.
Summary: An introduction to the life and behavior of bats.
ISBN-13: 978-1-56397-327-7
ISBN-10: 1-56397-327-8
1. Bats—Juvenile literature. [1. Bats.] I. Henderson, Meryl, ill.
II. Title.
599.4—dc21   1999   AC   CIP
98-83192

First edition
The publishers thank Barbara French of Bat Conservation International for reviewing the text and sketches for accuracy.
Edited by Harold D. Underdown
The text of this book is set in 16-point Clearface Regular.
The illustrations are done in watercolor.

10

2

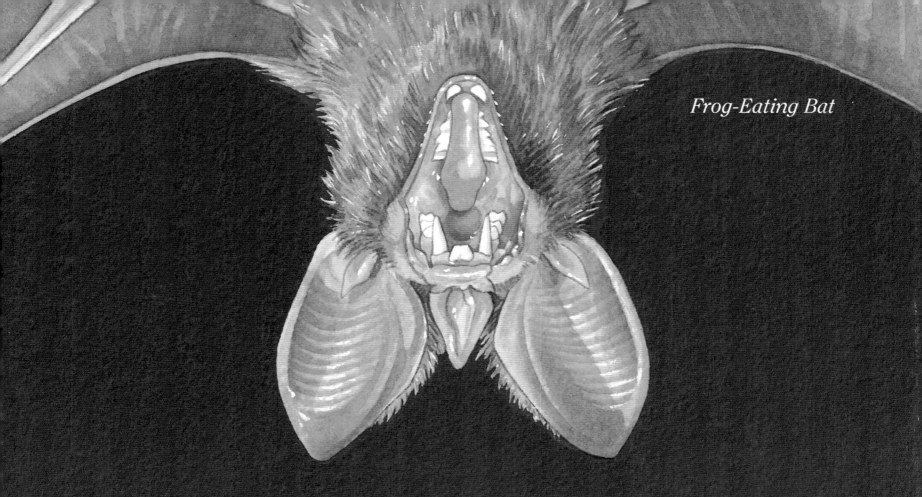

Frog-Eating Bat

If you were a bat, you could stay up all night. You could hang by your thumbs, or hang upside down by your toenails. You could fly through dark woods and even darker caves and not bump into anything.

If you were a bat, you would be afraid of people. A person, even a child, would look like a huge monster to you. When a bat is afraid it

The same bat looks quite different when it is calm and not afraid. And when people look calmly at bats, they can learn that bats are gentle, intelligent, and fascinating animals. Bats are among the most beneficial animals on earth.

Frog-Eating Bat

Gambian Epauleted Bat with young

Bats are mammals. Baby bats nurse milk from their mothers, just as human babies and mouse babies do. But bats are not mice with wings, as some people think. They are a special group of mammals—the only ones that fly. Bats are the masters of the night sky.

Almost a thousand kinds of bats live on earth. Bats live in tropical rain forests, in mountains, in deserts, and probably right in your neighborhood. Forty-four different kinds of bats live in North America.

Flying Foxes

Most bats live in the warm tropics. Among these are the megabats. "Mega" means large. They weigh up to four pounds, about half as much as a small cat. Megabats live in Asia, Africa, and Australia. They are called flying foxes.

Some megabats have mega-wings—up to six feet across when they fly. They also have mega-eyes—big eyes that allow them to see very well. With their keen eyesight and their sense of smell, flying foxes can find fruit or the nectar and pollen of flowers to eat.

As they feed and fly about, flying foxes help many tropical plants to reproduce. Seeds from the fruit that bats eat are spread far and wide. New trees grow from the seeds.

In East Africa, the flowers of the giant baobab tree open only at night. When bats take nectar from the flowers, they accidentally carry pollen from one flower to another. This helps the flowers produce seeds for new trees. Without bats, the baobab and many other tropical trees would die out.

Wahlberg's Epauleted Bat

In Mexico and the Southwestern United States, flowers of giant cactus plants also open at night. The lesser long-nosed bat laps up nectar from the flowers. By accident it also helps pollinate the cactus flowers.

The lesser long-nosed bat is a microbat. "Micro" means small. A microbat that lives in Thailand is the world's tiniest bat. It weighs less than a United States penny. Its body is about the size of a big bee, so it is called the bumblebee bat.

Bumblebee Bat (actual size)

10

Little Brown Bats

There are eight hundred kinds of microbats in the world. All bats in North America are microbats. If microbats live near your home, you are lucky. They are good neighbors. Most microbats eat flying insects, including mosquitoes and other insect pests.

The little brown bat is a microbat that lives in many parts of North America. It sleeps all day in an attic, a hollow tree, or other shelter. Then, at dusk, the little brown bat spreads its wings and flies into the night in search of insect food.

Little Brown Bat

Imagine trying to catch tiny insects in the dark! In an hour, however, a little brown bat can catch several hundred mosquitoes. Like most microbats, it has a special way of catching insects and of finding its way in the dark.

As the bat flies, it sends out many high-pitched calls. The sounds bounce off nearby objects and return as echoes the bat can hear. From the echoes, the bat is able to locate objects in front of it. This is called echolocation.

Scientists have made echolocation systems, but they are not nearly as good as those of bats. The echoes a bat receives give it a clear picture in its brain of what lies ahead. It is able to dodge twigs and even strands of very fine wire. The bat can tell the size, shape, and movement of a flying insect.

Noctule Bat

Bats are the athletic stars of the night sky. A bat can snatch a mosquito or moth from the air with its mouth. Or it can use its wing like a baseball player's glove to snag a bug and then bring the insect to its mouth.

When a bat is thirsty, it skims low over a pond or stream. It takes a sip of water on the wing. The gray bat even catches mayflies from the water's surface.

The greater bulldog bat of Central and South America grabs small fish out of the water. This microbat is often called the fishing bat. When echoes of its sounds bounce off a fish's back fin or from ripples in the water made by the fish, the bat zeroes in on its target. It clutches the fish in its claws. Its extra-sharp teeth grip the slippery fish. The fishing bat even has two cheek pouches for storing a fish until it finds a safe place to eat its catch.

Greater Bulldog Bat

Some insects can detect the echolocation calls of bats. When a bat is near, a moth may dive and zig and zag. Some manage to escape.

Certain kinds of bats catch some of their food without using echolocation. In a dark cave, they need to use echolocation to find their way. Outdoors, they sometimes hunt without it. The California leaf-nosed bat sees very well in dim light. Also, its big ears help the bat hear insects on the move. It flies slowly and grabs crickets, beetles, and caterpillars right off the ground or from plants.

California Leaf-Nosed Bat

The pallid bat of the deserts of western North America also has big ears. It also flies slowly or even waits on the ground and listens carefully. It may hear a cricket or scorpion on the move, or the many footsteps of a centipede. Then it pounces.

Pallid Bat

Other kinds of microbats eat unusual foods. Some catch frogs. Some catch small birds, mice, and even other small bats.

One of the most unusual bats does not actually catch any prey. Instead, the common vampire bat of Central and South America lands gently on a cow or other large mammal. Or it can land nearby and walk or hop over the ground to its prey. With its sharp teeth, it makes a little bite, then licks up the blood that flows. A vampire may drink half of its weight in one meal, but that's not much—the vampire is a small bat. It only weighs between one and two ounces.

Vampire bats are known to share food. Back in its hideout after feeding, a vampire will spit up some of its blood meal so a hungry or sick member of its colony can eat.

A Vampire Bat walking toward its prey

When daylight comes, bats need a roost—a safe place to sleep. Flying foxes often hang from high tree limbs, out in the open, but most bats roost in caves, mines, buildings, or hollow trees.

Flying Fox Bats at dusk

Some rain forest bats make their own shelters. They chew partway through the veins of several leaves, causing the leaves to droop. This forms a tent-like space in which a colony of bats sleep.

Peter's Tent-Making Bats

Honduran white bats roost in a tent made from one big leaf. Sunlight shining through the leaf casts a green light on the sleeping bats. They look like part of the leaf, and are hidden from snakes and other predators.

In central Texas, bats form the largest mammal colony on earth in a summer roosting place called Bracken Cave. The bats are microbats called Mexican free-tailed bats. In the spring, millions of female bats fly from Mexico to the cave. In June they each give birth to a single pup. This doubles the colony's numbers, to about 40 million.

At dusk, swirling clouds of bats rise nearly two miles high, catching winds that carry them to faraway insect hunting areas. Spreading over Texas towns and farms, the bats may eat as much as two hundred tons of insects each summer night.

Mexican Free-Tailed Bats

23

Mexican Free-Tailed Bats: mother and several pups

At night's end the female bats pour down from the sky. They zoom into Bracken Cave at sixty miles an hour. Both mothers and pups emit high-pitched squeaks. The dark cave is filled with fluttering bats and millions of bat voices. Yet, remarkably, each mother finds her pup.

She nurses it and licks its fur. Like cats, bats often groom themselves and each other. Within minutes of being born—even before it has fur—a bat pup begins to lick its wings.

Mexican Funnel-Eared Bats

In the fall, Mexican free-tailed bats fly to roosts in Mexico. Other bats also migrate hundreds of miles to a winter refuge. It is cold. There are no insects to eat. Many North American bats huddle together in a mine, cave, or other shelter and slip into a deep sleep called hibernation. A hibernating bat seems barely alive. It may only breathe twice in an hour.

If people disturb a colony of hibernating bats, the bats wake up and use some of their precious store of energy. Many bats die if they are awakened several times in the winter.

Sometimes colonies of bats lose their favorite roosting or hibernating place when the entrance to an abandoned mine is closed. People who care about bats are working to save such places. A strong "bat gate" can keep people out but give bats a safe home.

Little Brown Bats

At night, a bat's home is the sky. But in the day, in all seasons, a bat's survival depends on having a safe place to hide. Protecting these places is a goal of people who admire and appreciate bats. Some people even try to attract bats near their homes by putting up special bat roosting places.

They also tell their friends the truth about bats. Many people still have odd and incorrect ideas about bats. They believe that bats are ugly, disease-carrying creatures that are almost blind, and sometimes get entangled in women's hair.

By now you know that bats are not blind. Many bats see very well. Even those with the tiniest eyes see as well as mice. And any bat that can use echolocation to catch a moth zigzagging through the air can easily avoid getting tangled in someone's hair. The truth is, bats may swoop close to people at night. They are hunting insects. They may even catch a mosquito that was hunting a person!

Chapin's Free-Tailed Bat

Hammerhead Bat

False Vampire Bat

Sometimes a few bats out of many carry a dangerous disease called rabies. A bat that is dying from this disease can pass it on with a bite. But such a bat is still a gentle, shy creature that is afraid of people. To avoid danger, a wise rule is to never touch a bat.

Wrinkle-Faced Bat

Gothic Bat

Some bats do have strange-looking faces. They have some of the oddest-looking noses and ears in the animal world. Most of these features help bats receive echoes for their echolocation system. These features may look ugly but they work beautifully.

By eating insect pests and helping many valuable plants reproduce, bats themselves also fit beautifully in the natural world.

To Learn More About Bats

As recently as the middle of the twentieth century, most people in North America thought of the wolf as a big, "bad" animal. Then they gradually learned the truth about wolf behavior and the value of wolves in nature. Now the wolf is widely appreciated.

The same change is happening with bats. About 1975, bats were one of the least popular groups of animals on earth. Since then many people have learned that bats are "gentle friends, essential allies," as they are described in a booklet of Bat Conservation International. This organization has played a major role in public education about bats.

Many nature centers and science museums, as well as some state and national parks, offer field trips, workshops, and other programs about bats. If you are fortunate enough to have bats in your neighborhood, you can watch them hunt insects in the twilight. An inexpensive guide for identifying bats is the paperback *Bats of the World*, by Gary Graham (Golden Press, 1994.)

You may want to buy or build a shelter in which bats can rest in the daytime. Whether a bat house will attract bats depends on its design, color, and location. Bat Conservation International continues to study these factors and is the best source of up-to-date information.

Even the most enthusiastic advocates of bats do not encourage anyone to touch them. In some bat populations a small number of bats carry the disease rabies. Worldwide, 99 percent of all people who die of rabies get it from dogs, not bats. Still, do not touch a bat that appears to be injured or sick. Admire bats from a distance—for their well-being and your own.

For more information about bats, bat houses, and educational efforts to inform people about the value of bats, contact:

Bat Conservation International
Post Office Box 162603
Austin, Texas 78716-2603
(512) 327-9721
www.batcon.org